Table of Contents

QTP Basics

Record and playback

1. What are the modes of recording?

There are 3 types of recording modes.

- Analog Recording
- Low Level Recording
- Normal Recording

Add – in supported

1. What are the different add-ins' supported in QTP?

There are many add-ins' supported in QTP like web, Java, .Net,silverlight

2. What are the default add-ins' in QTP?
In QTP there are 3 default add-ins' viz. activex, visual basic,web

Licenses
1. What are the types of licenses in QTP?

There are 2 types of licences.

- Seat License
- Concurrent License

Test Settings in QTP

1. Explain Test Settings in QTP.

Test settings is very important part of the QTP test. You can open the test settings from the file sub menu.
You will find below sections in test settings window.

1. Properties Settings:

In properties section you will find the location of the test and add-ins associated with the test.

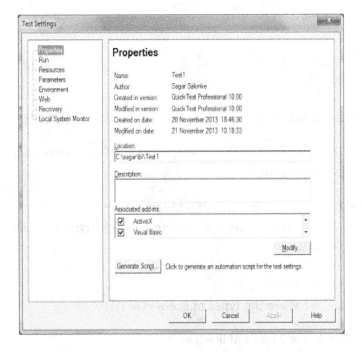

2. Run Settings:

In run section you will find below settings.

Data table iterations

When error occurs - what to do

Object Synchronization timeout

3. Resources Settings:

In resources section you will be able to see/edit the associated function libraries of the test.

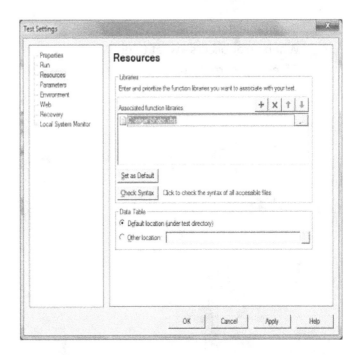

4. Parameters Settings:

In parameters section you will specify the input and ouptu parameters.

You can access the parameters using script as mentioned below.

Set qtApp = CreateObject("QuickTest.Application") ' Create the Application object
Set pDefColl = qtApp.Test.ParameterDefinitions
Set rtParams = pDefColl.GetParameters() ' Retrieve the Parameters collection defined for the test.
Set rtParam = rtParams.Item("sagar") ' Retrieve a

specific parameter.

print rtParam.value

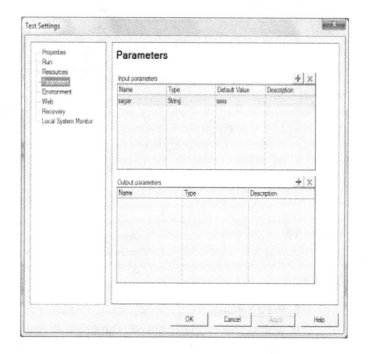

5. Environment Settings:

In Environment section you can view built - in and user defined global variables. You can also create new user defined variables here.

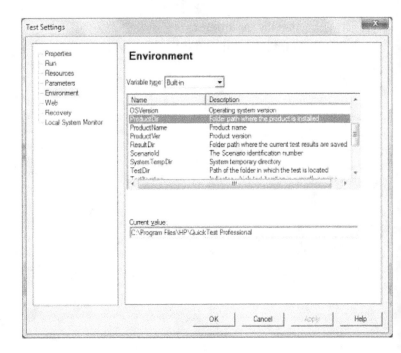

6. Web Settings:

In web section you can specify the browser navigation timeout.

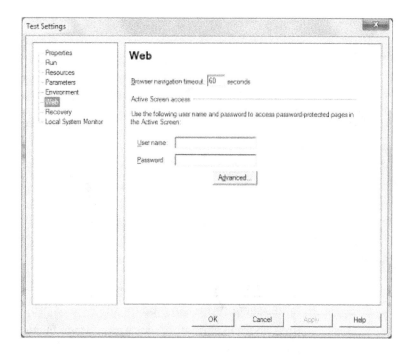

7. Recovery Settings:

In recovery section you will be able to add and activate/deactivate new recovery scenarios to the test. You can also view the properties of the scenarios.

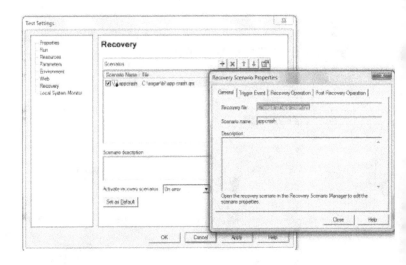

8. Local System Monitor Settings:

In this section you can monitor the various properties of the system like memory usage, cpu usage by given application during test execution.

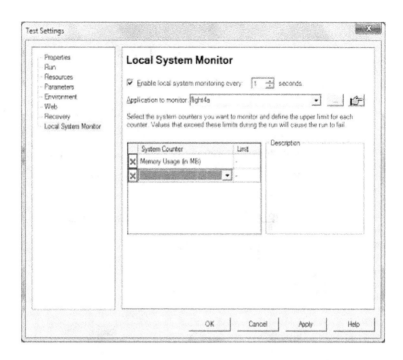

Checkpoints and Output Values

Checkpoints

Checkpoints are used to verify the property values with expected ones. If they match checkpoints pass else they fail. You can add standard checkpoint by right clicking the statement and then selecting the insert standard checkpoint menu.

Sample checkpoint window is shown in below fig.

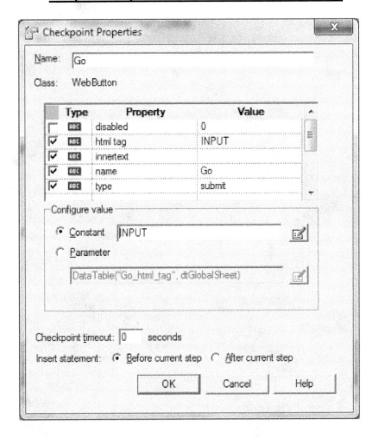

Browser("Google").Page("Google").WebEdit("q").Set "salunke"
Browser("Google").Page("Google").WebEdit("q").Check CheckPoint("q_2")
Browser("Google").Page("Google").WebEdit("q").Outpu t CheckPoint("q")
Browser("Google").Page("Google").WebButton("Google Search").Click

Output Values

Output value is used to store the data generated by application while execution is going on for later use. For example - Suppose after you place the order, order id is generated. So you can store this order id in output value so that you can use this value for later use to fax the order. To add the output value you have right click on the statement after which you want to add output value. Once you right click you will find the output value properties window like the one below.

You can check the property values that you want to store in the output value. You can also specify where you want to store the values (Data table or environment)

Browser("Google").Page("Google").WebEdit("q").Set "salunke"
Browser("Google").Page("Google").WebEdit("q").Output CheckPoint("q")
Browser("Google").Page("Google").WebButton("Google Search").Click

Object Repository

Local OR

1. **What is the Difference between local and shared object repository (OR) in QTP?**

   Object repository is used to store the test object and its properties/values. There are 2 types of Object Repositories.
   Local
   Shared
   Difference between local and shared OR is given below

   - Local OR is used by only one action in Test While Shared OR can be used by multiple actions and tests
   - Local OR can be edited without OR manager While shared OR can be edited by using only OR manager
   - We cannot merge 2 local OR but we can merge 2 shared ORs using OR manager
   - We cannot compare 2 local OR but we can compare 2 shared ORs using OR manager
   - We can associate/disassociate the shared OR to test at run time but Local OR is associated to test at any time by default.
   - Extension of the shared OR is .tsr while Local OR is .mtr
   - When we export the Local OR, shared OR is created.

Shared OR

1. What is the use of object repository manager in QTP?

Object repository manager in QTP is very important tool to manage the shared object repository. Please note that you can't use Object repository manager in QTP to manage local object repository.

Below are the main uses of Object repository manager in QTP.

- Open and edit shared object repository (TSR files).
- Compare 2 shared Object repositories in QTP.
- Merge 2 shared Object repositories in QTP.

2. How to Associate Object Repository to QTP Test?

Well - we can associate object repository to QTP Test either manually or by automation code.

Manually with Test Settings - In this method you have to go to Resources->Associate repositories. Here you can give the path of tsr file that is Shared OR.

By Automation Code, You have to use repositories collection object as mentioned in below code.

Dim QTPAPP
Dim qtObjRes

```
Set QTPAPP= CreateObject("QuickTest.Application")
QTPAPP.Launch
QTPAPP.Visible = True
QTPAPP.Open "C:\Test\Testabc", False, False
Set qtObjRes = QTPAPP.Test.Actions
("Login").ObjectRepositories
qtObjRes.Add "C:\OR\myRes.tsr", 1
```

3. How to create a Shared Object Repository in QTP?

Please follow the steps given below to create a shared
Object Repository in QTP.
Open Local Or
Go to File->Export Local Objects
Save file as abc.tsr
So abc.tsr will be a shared OR and we can associate it
with any test.

Descriptive Programming

Static

1. When to use descriptive Programming in QTP?

Descriptive programming in QTP is used in below scenarios.
Whenever the objects in the applications change quite often.
When it is not feasible to store the objects in OR. For example all links on the page
When same object exists in the different pages/windows of the application.

There are 2 types of description programming.
Static Descriptive programming
Dynamic Descriptive programming

Static Descriptive programming Example -

Browser("index:=0").page("title:=Google").webedit("name:=q").set "xyz"

Dynamic Descriptive programming Example -
'Find all edit boxes on google page using descriptive programming
Set descriptionObject = Description.Create()
descriptionObject("micclass").value = "webedit"
*descriptionObject("outerhtml").value = ".*input.*"*
descriptionObject("outerhtml").regularexpression = true

set col =

```
Browser("index:=0").page("title:=Google").childobjects(
descriptionObject)
print "Total edit boxes on the page" & col.count
For i=0 to col.count-1
 print col(i).getROProperty("outerhtml")
Next
```

Dynamic

1. **How to use regular expression in descriptive programming in QTP?**

   As we know that there are 2 ways of descriptive programming.
   Static
   Dynamic
   We can use regular expression in both the ways as mentioned below. Please note that by default all the property values are considered as regular expressions by QTP.
   <u>Regular Expressions in Static descriptive programming in QTP.</u>

   ```
   Browser("index:=0").page("title:=Google").Webedit("na
   me:=q").set "sagar salunke"
   Browser("creationtime:=0").page("title:=Google").Webb
   utton("name:=Google.*").Click
   ```

   Please note that last statement uses regular expression to identify the button whose name starts with Google. If your property value itself contains the special character then that should be escaped using \

character.

Example - Suppose you want to click on the link "+sagar".
Now this link contains the special character +. To click on this link, we can use below code
Browser("creationtime:=0").page("title:=Google").Link(" innertext:=\+sagar").Click

Regular Expressions in Dynamic descriptive programming in QTP.

Set descriptionObject = Description.Create()
descriptionObject("innertext").value = "+sagar"
descriptionObject("innertext").RegularExpression = false

'Please note that we can specify whether the value is regular expression or not using RegularExpression property. By default it is true.

Browser("index:=0").page("title:=Google").Link(descripti onObject).click

This is how we can use Regular Expressions in QTP

Recovery Scenario Manager

Recovery Scenario Wizard

1. What are the steps in creating recovery scenario?

Open Recovery Scenario Manager.Using recovery
scenario manager you can create new recovery
scenarios and store it in a file with .qrs extension. One
qrs file may contain multiple recovery scenarios. To
create new recovery scenario, click on the button
circled with red color. It will open recovery scenario
wizard.

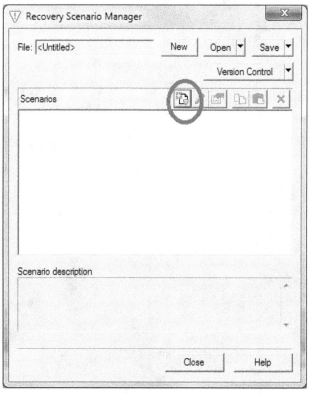

Open Recovery Scenario Wizard.Recovery scenario wizard shows the steps involved in creating the recovery scenario. Click on Next

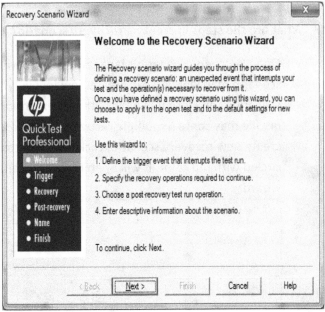

Select Trigger Event.There are 4 types of the trigger events.

Pop up window

Object State

Test Run Error

Application Crash

Specify the trigger Details. In this step you have to specify more details about the trigger. For example if you selected pop up window in trigger event above, you will have to provide the title or text of the pop up as shown below.

Recovery Operation. After specifying the trigger event, you have to provide the recovery operation. There are 4 types of the recovery operations.

Keyboard or mouse operation

Close application process

Function Call

Restart Microsoft Windows

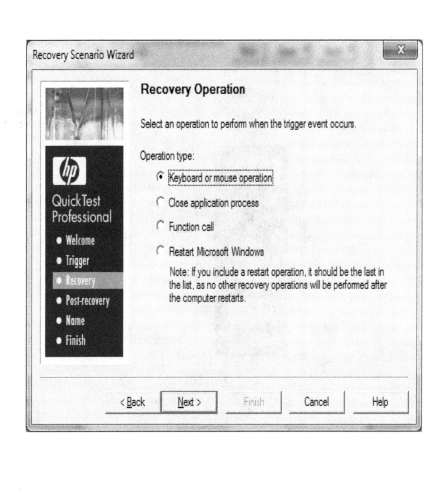

Post Recovery Operation.

In Post Recovery You can tell what step should be
executed after recovery is done by QTP.

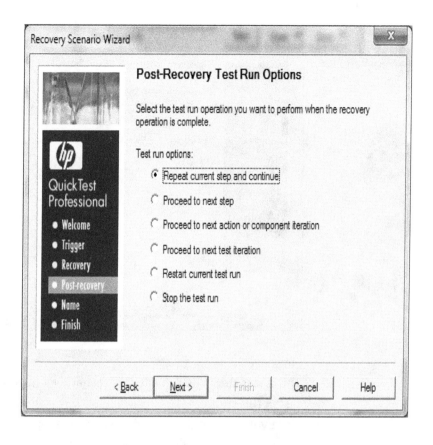

Name the Recovery Scenario.

You have to give the name to recovery scenario in this step

Finishing the recovery scenario.

This is last step. You can add this scenario to current test in this step.

Once you click finish recovery scenario manager window will be shown where you can save the qrs file. Please note that to activate recovery scenario, you have to go to test settings.

Excel and Data tables in QTP

Excel

1. How to import excel sheet to data table in qtp?

When we design a test automation framework in qtp, we usually store the test data inside excel sheets. Sometimes we need to load the test data in datatable to execute the test cases.

We can either import all excel sheets from excel workbook or we can import particular excel sheet from the the workbook to the datatable

To import all sheets from excel file, use below line of code
datatable.Import "c:\abc.xls"

To import single sheet from excel file, use below line of code
'here we are importing the sheet global from abc.xls into testdata sheet in Data table in QTP.

datatable.AddSheet "testdata"
datatable.ImportSheet "c:\abc.xls","Global","testdata"

2. How to read a value from Excel cell in QTP?

Below script will read data from excel file

```
filepath  = "C:\Bugs\Report.xlsx"
Set objExcel  = createObject("Excel.Application")
objExcel.Visible = True
Set Wb = objExcel.Workbooks.Open(filepath)
print Wb.worksheets(1).Cells(1,1).Value
```

Data tables

1. How to export datatable to excel Sheet?

Add some data to global sheet in datatable
datatable.GlobalSheet.AddParameter "p1","v"
datatable("p1") = "abc"

Export complete datatable - This will export all sheets
from the datatable
datatable.Export("c:\abc.xls")

Export only particular sheet from the datatable to excel
sheet
After below code is executed, sheet with name global
will be exported to excel
sheet in kk.xls

datatable.ExportSheet "c:\kk.xls","Global"

Databases in QTP

Microsoft Access

1. How to get data from the access data base in QTP?

Code below can be used to read data from database in QTP.

```
Set db = createobject("ADODB.Connection")
db.Open "Provider=Microsoft.Jet.OLEDB.4.0;Data
Source=G:\priyanka\vb6\admission_project.mdb;Persist
Security Info=False"

Set rst = createobject("ADODB.Recordset")
rst.Open "select * from Course ", db,3

id = rst.RecordCount
For i=0 to id-1
    print rst.fields(0) & rst.fields(1) & rst.fields(2) &
rst.fields(3)
    rst.Movenext
Next
```

2. How to insert a record or data into database in qtp?

Code below can be used to insert data into database in QTP.

```
Set cn= createobject("ADODB.Connection")
```

```
cn.Open "Provider=Microsoft.Jet.OLEDB.4.0;Data
Source=G:\priyanka\vb6\admission_project.mdb;Persist
Security Info=False"
Set rst = createobject("ADODB.Recordset")
cn.execute "insert into table(column1,column2) values
(colvalue1,colvalue2)"
```

Utility Objects in QTP

Reporter

1. Explain Reporter Object in QTP.

Reporter object is used to log the pass/fail status of the step to the results.
We can use below syntax for logging the results.

Reporter.ReportEvent EventStatus, ReportStepName, Details [, ImageFilePath]

DotNetFactory

1. Explain DotNetFactory Object in QTP.

In QTP, you can use dotnetfactory object to access .net objects. You must have .net framework installed in your system before you use createinstance method.
It enables you to create an instance of a .NET object, and access its methods and properties. Createinstance method returns a COM interface for a .NET object.

Syntax
Set myobj = DotNetFactory.CreateInstance (TypeName [,Assembly] [,args])

Here
Typename - any type name that .net framework provides

Example

The following example uses the CreateInstance method to create a object of a system environment type

Set obj =
Dotnetfactory.CreateInstance("System.Environment")
print obj.MachineName

File Handling in QTP

Files

1. How to read a text file in QTP?

How to Read a text file in QTP
Example -
Below code will Read a text file in QTP

```
Set fso = CreateObject("Scripting.FileSystemObject")
Set f = fso.OpenTextFile("c:\mytestfile.txt", 1)
print  f.ReadAll
```

Above code will read all data from c:\mytestfile.txt file
and print it in QTP.

2. How to create a text file in QTP?

Below Code will create a text file in QTP

```
Set fso = CreateObject("Scripting.FileSystemObject")
Set MyFile = fso.CreateTextFile("d:\mytestfile.txt", True)
MyFile.WriteLine("This is my  test.")
MyFile.Close
```

This is how we can create a text file in QTP.

3. How to write contents to text file in QTP

Example -

Below Code will write all data in contents variable to text file in QTP

```
content = "This will be in file "
Set Fo = createobject("Scripting.FilesystemObject")
Set f = Fo.openTextFile("c:\abc.txt",8,true)
f.Write (contents)
f.Close
Set f = nothing
```

Folders

1. **How to create a folder in QTP?**

   Below code will create a folder in QTP

```
Environment.Value("ResultFolderPath") = "C:\myf"
Set Fo = createobject("Scripting.FilesystemObject")
If Not
Fo.FolderExists(Environment.Value("ResultFolderPath"))
Then
        Fo.CreateFolder (
Environment.Value("ResultFolderPath") )
End If
```

Web applications and HTML DOM in QTP

1. How to Use HTML DOM in QTP?

Using html DOM you extract all kind of information from web page as you can access source code of the page in the form of HTML.

HTML DOM has many method and properties associated with it like getElementById, nextsibling etc. To access these methods you must create the DOM object first.

Set domObject = Browser("myb").Page("myp").object

Above statement will create the DOM object for the page called myp.
Now let us use the dom object we have created above to get more information of the page currently displayed in the application.

Print domObject.getElementById("myid").innerText
' Prints the text inside the Element - myid
Print domObject.getElementById("myid").innerHTML
' Prints the inner HTML of Element - myid

4. How to access the parent object of given DOM Object

You can also find the parentobject, nextsibling, previoussibling of the given dom object using built in properties as mentioned below.

Set parentObj =
domObject.getElementById("myid").parentNode ' gets
the parent object of myid
Set nextsiblingObj =
domObject.getElementById("myid").nextsibling 'gets the
next sibling object of myid
Set previoussiblingObj =
domObject.getElementById("myid").previoussibling

For complete list of methods you can
visit http://www.w3schools.com/jsref/dom
_obj_node.asp

5. **How to get the collection of all TD (table data cells) elements of the table using HTML DOM in QTP?**

   Set tdtags
   =Browser("a").Page("p").WebTable("t").Object.getElem
   entsByTagName("TD")

6. **How to get the collection of all TH (table header cells) elements of the table using HTML DOM in QTP?**

   set thtags =
   Browser("abc").Page("mypage").WebTable("mytable").
   Object.getElementsByTagName("TH")

7. **How to get the value of attribute of any element using HTML DOM in QTP?**

   Set myobj =
   Browser("abc").Page("mypage").WebTable("mytable").
   Object
   Print myobj.getAttribute("class")

*'This will print the value of class attribute of myobj -
table*

8. **How to get the collection of all table rows using HTML DOM in QTP?**

    *Set tableObj
    =Browser("abc").Page("mypage").WebTable("mytable")
    .Object
    Set trtags = tableObj.getElementsByTagName("tr")*

9. **How to find the total number of rows in table Using HTML DOM in QTP?**

    print trtags.length

10. **How to get the value inside table cell Using HTML DOM in QTP?**

    *Set tdtags
    =Browser("abc").Page("mypage").WebTable("mytable")
    .Object.getElementsByTagName("TD")*

    *Print tdtags(0).innerText
    'print the text displayed inside first td tag in table*

11. **What is previousSibling, nextSibling in QTP?**

    Well - let me tell you that all the properties
    (previousSibling, nextSibling) are not defined by QTP.

    All these properties are HTML DOM properties that help
    us get the elements at the same level of the given
    element in web page.

You can access these method in QTP using .object
property which lets you access native methods and
properties of the objects/elements.

Example -

```
<body>
<div id="parentdiv">
 This text is inside div element of which id is - parentdiv

<div id="fc">
 This is nested div1
</div>


<div id="sc">
 This is nested div2.
</div>


</div>
</body>
```

As you can see in above example, 2 div elements (fc, sc)
are inside the div(parentdiv).
So for fc-div and sc-div, parentdiv is the parent element.
While for parentdiv, fc-div and sc-div are child div
elements. The div elements fc-div and sc-div are siblings
of each other as both are at same level.
sc-div is the nextSibling of the fc-div. While fc-div is the
previousSibling of the sc-div.

You can get access to these elements using HTML DOM
properties nextSibling, previousSibling properties

For example -
'access the next sibling of fc-div
set obj=
Browser("myb").Page("myp").object.getElementById("fc
")
print obj.nextSibling.innerText

'access the previous Sibling of sc-div
set obj=
Browser("myb").Page("myp").object.getElementById("sc
")
print obj.previousSibling.innerText

12. What is parentNode, childNodes, firstChild, lastChild in QTP?

Well - let me tell you that all the properties
(parentNode, childNodes, firstChild, lastChild) are not
defined by QTP.

All these properties are HTML DOM properties that help
us get the child and parent element of the given
element in web page.

You can access these method in QTP using .object
property which lets you access native methods and
properties of the objects/elements.

Example -

```
<body>
<div id="parentdiv">
 This text is inside div element of which id is - parentdiv

<div id="fc">
 This is nested div1
</div>


<div id="sc">
 This is nested div2.
</div>


</div>
</body>
```

As you can see in above example, 2 div elements (fc, sc) are inside the div(parentdiv).
So for fc-div and sc-div, parentdiv is the parent element.
While for parentdiv, fc-div and sc-div are child div elements.

You can get access to these elements using HTML DOM properties parentNode, childNodes, firstChild, lastChild.

For example -
```
'access the child objects
set divParentObject=
```

```
Browser("myb").Page("myp").object.getElementById("p
arentdiv")
print divParentObject.firstChild.innerText
print divParentObject.lastChild.innerText

set allchilds = divParentObject.childNodes
for i=0 to allchilds.length-1
 print allchilds(i).innerText
next

'access the parent element of div with id "fc"
set childObject =
Browser("myb").Page("myp").object.getElementById("fc
")

print childObject.parentNode.innerText
```

13. What is getElementsByTagName in QTP?

If you are testing web application, you may have used getElementsByTagName method to get access to all elements that have given tag.

Please note that this is not QTP's own method but it is native HTML DOM method.

getElementsByTagName takes one parameter as an input which should be the tag of the element like td, tr, span, div etc.
This method returns the collection of elements that have the given tagname.

Example.

```
<body>
<div id="head">
This text is inside div element of which id is - head
</div>

<div>
This is another div
</div>

<div>
This is div number 3.
</div>

</body>
```

In above example, we have sample html document body in which there are 3 div elements.

To get the text value inside all these div elements, we can use the innertext method as mentioned below.

```
set tn =
Browser("myb").Page("myp").object.getElementsByTag
Name("DIV")
for i=0 to tn.length-1
  'print the innertext of each div element here
   print tn(i).innerText
next
```

Thus basically we use getElementsByTagName method to get all element objects with given tag name.

14. How to use getElementById in QTP?

I know that you have come on this page because you are testing the web application.
Web application testing is very interesting stuff.

Apart from normal web methods and properties provided by QTP, you can use lot of native methods of the web elements.

One of such native method of the document object is getElementById.
This method takes one parameter as an input which should be the id of the element.

Example.

```
<body>
<div id="head">
 This text is inside div element of which id is - head
</div>
</body>
```

In above example, we have sample html document body in which there is one div element with id = 'head' and it contains some text.

To get the value inside this div element, we can use the innertext method as mentioned below.

print
Browser("myb").Page("myp").object.getElementById("h
ead").innerText

So output of above code will be.

"This text is inside div element of which id is - head"

Thus basically we use getElementById method to get
the element object and then we can use its innerText
method to get the data inside that element.

Please note that we can also get the data inside hidden
elements using this method. QTP can not read data
inside hidden elements.

15. How to get innerText of webelement in QTP?

In my 10 years of experience in QTP, I have worked on
many web applications that involved jquery, ajax and
rich controls.

To test such applications we must have good
understanding of the HTML DOM concept.
Extracting the values from the web elements on the
page is very common thing that we do in QTP.

To get the inner text or inner html of the web elements,
we can use below syntax.

Example -

print

browser("bb").page("xys").Object.getElementById("pqr").innerText

Please note that we should use the .object after property before we use html dom.

In above example I am trying to get the text displayed inside web element of which id is "pqr"

We can use more such methods as mentioned below to get access to the web elements on the page
1. getElementById()   - get the element by id
2. getElementsByTagName() - get all elements with given tag name
3. getElementsByClassName() - (does not work in < ie9) - get all elements having given class
4. getAttribute() - get the value of attribute of given node
5. getAttributeNode() - get the attribute node
6. hasAttribute() - check if a node has given attribute
7. hasChildNodes() - check of node has any children
8. item() - access the node based on the index from the collection

Once we get the element object, we can use below properties to get the data.
1. innerHTML – gets the html code inside element
2. innerText - gets the text value inside element
3. getAttribute – gets the value of attribute
4. nodeName - (like TD, SPAN, #text, #document, Attribute name)

5. nodeType   - (Element, Text, Attribute, Comment, Document)
6. nodeValue - (attribute Value)
7. childNodes   - gets all child elements of the given node
8. attributes   - gets the collection of all attributes of given node
9. className   - gets the name of class of given element
10. firstChild   - gets the access to first child element of the given node.
11. Id – gets the id of the given node.
12. lastChild – gets the last child element of the given node
13. nextSibling – gets the next element at the same level as given node.
14. offsetLeft
15. offsetTop
16. previousSibling - – gets the previous element at the same level as given node.
17. parentNode –gets the parent node of the given node
18. scrollLeft
19. scrollTop
20. scrollWidth
21. style   - gets the style information of the given node
22. tagName – gets the name of the tag of given node
23. textContent – gets the text displayed inside given node
24. title - gets the title of the given node
25. length – gets the total number of nodes in the collection.

This is how we can use html dom in qtp to get the information displayed on the webpage. This makes the web application testing quite easy stuff.

Framework Designing in QTP

Types of frameworks

1. What are the types of automation frameworks in QTP?

Types of Automation Frameworks in QTP
Automation framework is designed to ease the process of test automation using QTP. Automation framework helps from scalability point of view. It is very easy to automate the test cases using automation framework rather than ad hoc approach.

There are mainly 3 types of Automation Frameworks in QTP

- Keyword Driven Framework

- Data Driven Framework

- Hybrid Framework

Keyword Driven Framework :
In Keyword Driven Framework , Importance is given to functions than Test Data. when we have to test multiple functionality we can go for keyword frameworks. Each keyword is mapped to function in QTP library and application.

DATA Driven Framework :
In data driven framework, importance is given to test data than multiple functionality of application. We design data driven framework to work with applications

where we want to test same flow with different test data.

Hybrid Framework -
This is the combination of keyword and data driven frameworks.

After analyzing the application, you can decide what kind of framework best suits your needs and then you can design automation framework in QTP.

Components of framework
1. **Explain keyword driven automation framework in QTP?**

Keyword driven Automation Framework is most popular QTP framework. It is very easy to design and learn a keyword driven automation framework in QTP.

In this article I will explain you all details about how we can design and use keyword driven automation framework in QTP with example. I will also explain the advantages and disadvantages of keyword driven automation framework in QTP.
In keyword driven automation framework, focus is mainly on kewords/functions and not the test data. This means we focus on creating the functions that are mapped to the functionality of the application.

For example - Suppose you have a flight reservation application which provides many features like

- Login to the application
- Search Flights
- Book Flight tickets
- Cancel Tickets
- Fax Order
- View Reports

To implement the keyword driven automation framework for this kind of application we will create functions in vbscript for each functionality mentioned above. We pass the test data and test object details to these functions.

The main components of keyword driven automation framework in QTP

Each keyword driven automation framework has some common components as mentioned below.

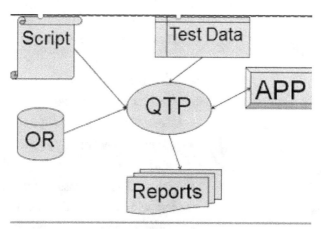

As dispalyed in above image, We have 5 main components in **keyword driven automation framework**

1. Scripts Library (.vbs, .txt, .qfl)
2. OR - Object Repository
3. Test Data (generally in excel format)
4. QTP - Settings and Environment Variables
5. Reports - (Generally in HTML format)
6. Test Driver Script/ Test Engine

2. Please explain how Test Data sheet looks like in keyword driven automation framework in QTP.

Generally automated test cases are stored in excel sheets. From QTP ,we read excel file and then row by row we execute the functions in a test case. Each test case is implemented as a set of keywords.
Common columns in Data sheet are mentioned below.

- Test case ID - Stores the Test Case ID mapped to Manual Test Cases.
- Test Case Name - Name of the Test cases/ Scenario.
- Execute Flag - if Marked Y -> Test case will be executed
- Test_Step_Id - Steps in a test case
- Keyword - Mapped to function in library file.
- Object Types - Class of the object e.g winedit, webedit, swfbutton etc
- Object Names -Names of objects in OR .
- Object Values - Actual test data to be entered in the objects.

- Parameter1 - This is used to control the execution flow in the function.

Test_ID	TC_Name	Execute	Test_Step_ID	Keyword	Object_Types	Object_Names	Object_Values	Parameter1
1	Login To App	Y	Step1	login	winedit;winedit	userid;password	salunke;mercury	
			Step2	Insert_Order	wincombobox;wincombobo	flyfrom;flyto	london;paris	
			Step3	Fax_Order				Order_Id

Please note that this is just a sample data sheet that can be used in keyword driven framework. There could be customized data sheets for each project depending upon the requirement and design.

For example there could be more parameters or test data is stored in the databases.

16. Please explain Test Driver Script in QTP.

This is the heart of keyword driven / data driven frameworks. This is the main script that interacts with all modules mentioned above.

Main tasks that are accomplished by driver script are ->

- Read data from the Environment variables /File or from ini file.
- Call report module to create Report folders / files
- Import Excel sheet to Data table.
- Read Excel file.
- Call the function mapped to keyword.
- Log the result

Error Handling and debugging in QTP

Error Handling

1. How to do Error Handling in QTP?

There are 2 ways in which we can handle errors in QTP.

- Err object.
- Recovery Scenarios.

Sample code to handle the error is given below

If err.number <> 0 Then
print err.description
else
print "there was no error in above statement"
end if

Whenever any error occurs in the script, We get the message window with detailed description of the error.

But when we are executing the scripts, we do not want this message box to appear to come as this will halt the execution of the script.

To prevent message box from appearing, we use below statement above the block of code.

On error resume next

----

more statements

With On error resume next in place, QTP script runs
even though error exists in the code. We can capture
those errors using Err object as stated earlier.

When you are debugging the scripts, you should not use
On error resume next statement as it will suppress the
errors and you will not be able to figure out the issue in
your script.Sample code to handle the error is given
below

If err.number <> 0 Then
print err.description
else
print "there was no error in above statement"
end if

Whenever any error occurs in the script, We get the
message window with detailed description of the error.

But when we are executing the scripts, we do not want
this message box to appear to come as this will halt the
execution of the script.

To prevent message box from appearing, we use below
statement above the block of code.

On error resume next

----

more statements

With *On error resume next* in place, QTP script runs even though error exists in the code. We can capture those errors using Err object as stated earlier.

When you are debugging the scripts, you should not use On error resume next statement as it will suppress the errors and you will not be able to figure out the issue in your script.

QTP and VbScript

1. When do we use Cdate and Cstr in QTP?

Cdate and Cstr are data type conversion functions in QTP.

For Example -

CDATE

DOB = "09-jan-1986"
myDate = CDate(DOB)

myDate will have date data type.

Cstr

a = 10
mystring = cstr (a)

mystring will have data type as String....

17. Explain DateDiff function in QTP.

DateDiff function is used to find out the difference between 2 dates.

For example -
Suppose you know the date of birth of someone and want to find out the age of that person, you can use datediff function in this case.

DateDiff (Interval_Type, Date1, Date2)

Here Interval Type can be of below types.

yyyy - Year

m - Month

d - Day

h - Hour

n - Minute

s - Second

Example -

dateofbirth ="09-01-1986"

print datediff("yyyy", dateofbirth ,now)

'This will print your age in years

18. What are the different String functions in QTP?

Here is the list of all string functions in QTP.

String functions to extract the part of the string -

- **left** - gets the specified number of characters from the left side of string
- **mid** -gets the specified number of characters from the given position of the string
- **right** - gets the specified number of characters from the right side of string

String functions to remove the spaces from the string -

- **ltrim** - removes the blank spaces from the left side of the string

- **rtrim** - removes the blank spaces from the right side of the string
- **trim** - removes the blank spaces from the left and right side of the string

Other String functions -

- **String** - Returns a string of the given length with specified character.
- **Space** - Returns the empty string with given length
- **strReverse** - Reverses the given string
- **ucase** - Converst the string to upper case
- **lcase** - Converts the string to lower case
- **strComp** - Compares 2 strings
- **replace** - replaces the given string str1 from input string say str with other string say str2
- **len** - gets the number of characters in given string
- **split** - splits the string into array using given delimiter
- **join** - forms the string from given array elements
- **cstr** - converts the data type of the variable into String
- **chr** - gets the character corresponding to the given ascii value
- **Asc** - gets the ascii value of the given character.
- **instr** - searches for a substring in a given string and returns the position where the match is found.
- **InStrRev**- searches for a substring in a given string and returns the position where the match is found from the end of the string.

19. Explain replace function in QTP with Example.

Replace function is used to replace the part of the given string with other sub string in QTP.

Example -

myString = "Sachin plays cricket"

print replace(myString,"Sachin","Dhoni")
'Will print Dhoni plays cricket

print replace(myString,"sachin","Dhoni")
'Will print Sachin plays cricket. Because we have used sachin in small case letter

print replace(myString,"sachin","Dhoni",1,-1,0)
'Will print Sachin plays cricket .....Same as above

print replace(myString,"sachin","Dhoni",1,-1,1)
'Will print Dhoni plays cricket....
'The last parameter of replace determines whether the replacement is case-sensitive or case-insensitive.
'If last parameter is 0, replacement is case-sensitive
'If last parameter is 1, replacement is case-insensitive

Syntax -

replace(myString,"replacethis","replacewith",startat,count,comparisonmehtod)

Parameter1 - myString - > String to be scanned and modified
Parameter2 - replacethis- > String to be searched and replaced for
Parameter3 - replacewith- > String to be replaced with
Parameter4 - startat- > from what position the myString should be searched...Default is 1.
Parameter5 - count- > How many replacements should be done. Default is -1 - All occurrences
Parameter6 - comparisonmehtod- > Is comparison case-sensitive?..Default is 0 - binary comparison.

20. Explain right, mid, left functions in QTP with Examples.

QTP supports lot of string functions.
Some of the commonly used string manipulation functions are given below.
- right
- mid
- left

All of the above functions are frequently used when performing any string operations in QTP.
All of the above functions extract the part of the string / Sub string.

Right function returns the fixed number of characters from right side of the string.
Left function returns the fixed number of characters from left side of the string.

Mid function can be used to get the characters/ sub string from the left, right or middle part of the string.

Examples -

myString = "Sachin Plays Cricket"

print right(myString,7)
'will return the 7 characters from the right side of myString
'Cricket
print left(myString,6)
'will return the 6 characters from the left side of myString
'Sachin
print mid(myString,8,5)
'will return the 5 characters from the 8th position of myString
'Plays

Syntax -
Second parameter in left and right function tells how many characters to return from the string.
In mid functions there are 2 parameters. First parameter tells from which position of the string we have to get the characters and second parameter tells how many characters to return.

21. Explain Ubound function in QTP.

Ubound stands for upper bound. This functions is used to find the upper bound of the array.

Syntax -

ubound(arrayname, dimension)

It returns the upper bound of the arrayname and dimension used is specified in second parameter. By default dimension is 1.

Example -

Single dimension array

Dim a(2)
'Declare an array with upper bound (index) as 2.

a(0) = 0
a(1) = 0
a(2) = 0

print ubound (a)   *'will print 2*
print ubound (a,1)   *'will print 2*

'This will print the value 2 as upper bound of the array is 2.

22. How to create a array of dictionary in QTP?

In QTP and vbscript we can create array of dictionary using below syntax/ example.

dim ArrayofDictionary(2)

'Now let us make first element of array as dictionary

Set ArrayofDictionary(0)=
createobject("scripting.dictionary")
ArrayofDictionary(0).Add "key1", "temp1"
ArrayofDictionary(0).Add "key2", "temp2"

'Added keys in first dictionary

'Now let us make second element of array as dictionary

Set ArrayofDictionary(1)=
createobject("scripting.dictionary")
ArrayofDictionary(1).Add "key1", "temp1"
ArrayofDictionary(1).Add "key2", "temp2"

'Added keys in second dictionary

and so on ....

To access the values inside dictionary, use below syntax.

print ArrayofDictionary(1)("key2")

23. How to remove the spaces from string in QTP

Example -

To remove the spaces from string in QTP, you can use replace function.

print replace(" sdsd sd sd s "," ","")

' Output will be sdsdsdsds

If you want to remove only leading spaces from string then you can use ltrim function

print ltrim(" sdsd sd s ")
'Output will be "sdsd sd s "

If you want to remove only trailing spaces from string then you can use rtrim function

print rtrim(" sdsd sd s ")
'Output will be " sdsd sd s"

24. What is early binding and late binding in QTP

In QTP, all variables of variant type. Meaning It is not necessary to declare a variable with any data type like int, float etc.

When we initialize a variable with any value, QTP will assign a data type to that variable depending upon what kind of Value is assigned to the variable.

Example -

Dim a
a = 10

' In above code, when we assign the value of 10 to a,

data type of a becomes integer.
This means that at runtime, the data type binding is happening. This is called as a late binding in QTP.

25. how to find yesterday's date in QTP?

Below code will find out yesterday's date in qtp .

```
print DateAdd("d",-1,date)
```

Please note that you can find any past or future date using above function. The second parameter is used to specify the interval number.

For example - If you specify 1, it will give you tomorrow's date. If you specify -2, it will give you the date one day before yesterday.

Miscellaneous Questions in QTP

This chapter will cover some other questions on QTP.

1. **How to send an email from Outlook in QTP?**

    Code mentioned below will send mail to aTO from outlook.

    Set Outlook = CreateObject("Outlook.Application")
    Dim Message 'As Outlook.MailItem
    Set Message = Outlook.CreateItem(olMailItem)
    With Message
    > *.Subject = Subject*
    > *.HTMLBody = TextBody*
    > *.Recipients.Add (aTo)*
    > *Const olOriginator = 0*
    > *.Send*

    End With

2. **How to use Regular Expressions in OR in QTP?**

    Object repository stores the test object properties and their values. We can use regular expressions to set the values of the properties of the test object.

    When we use the value as a regular expression, single test object in OR can be be used to find the multiple run time objects.

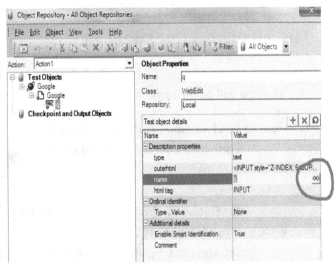

For Example -

As shown in above image, we need to click on the button (circled with red) in front of the property value that you want to make as a regular expression. After you click that button, you will get below window

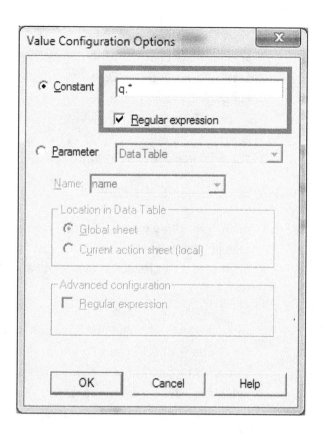

Then we need to enter the regular expression in the edit box and check the regular expression checkbox and click on Ok.

So now the test object will identify all the edit boxes that starts with q followed by any characters.

3. **How to read XML file in QTP?**

Set objXMLDoc =
CreateObject("Microsoft.XMLDOM")
objXMLDoc.async = False

```
objXMLDoc.load("books.xml")
Set parentel= objXMLDoc.documentElement
Set cList = parentel.getElementsByTagName("book")
For Each E In cList
    print E.Text
Next
```
This example will print all xml node values in QTP.

3. How to take a screenshot in QTP?

In QTP, when we execute the test cases, test cases may fail due to valid / invalid defects. They may also fail due to script issues or any other issues like network failure.

After the test execution ends, We only have the html reports or QTP results with us which does not give clear picture about the status of application. To solve this problem we can take the snapshot of the application when any test step fails.

Example - Below code will take the screen shot. You can insert this code anywhere you want to take the screen shot.

```
Window("xyz").CaptureBitmap
"c:\screenshots\abc.png",True
```
'In above code we are storing the png image file to c drive location. Second parameter tells whether to overwrite existing file.

Thus you can use capturebitmap method of any object to take the screen shot.

4. Dictionary Object in QTP with Example

Dictionary object is used to store the data in key-item pairs in qtp.

A Dictionary object is just like an associative array. It stores the data in the form of key-item pairs. Each key has some data item associated with it. Key can be integer or string format. Data item can be integer or string or array of variants. It may contain other dictionary itself.

Methods of Dictionary Object

Add -------> Adds new key-item pair in the dictionary object

Exists ----> returns true if the given key exists in the dictionary object

Items -----> returns the array containing all items in the dictionary object

Keys ------> returns the array containing all keys in the dictionary object

Remove ----> removes the key-item pair with given key from the dictionary object

RemoveAll -> removes all key-item pairs from the dictionary object

Properties of Dictionary Object

Count--------> returns the total number of keys in the dictionary object

Item---------> assigns or returns the item value with given key from the dictionary object
Key----------> sets the new key value for the given key
CompareMode -> assigns or returns the comparison mode for comparing string keys in a Dictionary object.

Example with dictionary object in QTP

```
'create new dictionary object
Set dictionaryObject =
CreateObject("Scripting.Dictionary")

'add some key-item pairs
dictionaryObject.Add "1", "Sagar"
dictionaryObject.Add "2", "Amol"
dictionaryObject.Add "3", "Ganesh"

'Display data in the dictionary
for each k in dictionaryObject.keys

 print k & " - " & dictionaryObject.item(k)

next


'Remove the key-item pair with key = 1  from the
dictionary object
dictionaryObject.Remove("1")

'Remove all key-item pairs from the dictionary
```

object
dictionaryObject.RemoveAll

'Release the object
Set dictionaryObject = nothing

5. Explain RegExp Object in QTP.

RegExp is a very important object in QTP that can be used to find the patterns in given string using regular expressions.

This object can be created using below syntax.
Set regExpObject = New RegExp

RegExp Object supports below properties.

Global Property - a pattern should match all occurrences in string or just the first one
IgnoreCase Property - specifies if the search is case-sensitive or not
Pattern Property - Sequence of literal characters and special characters (Meta Characters like *,?,+,\b,\d,\n etc)

RegExp Object supports below methods.

Test Method - returns true if the pattern is found in the given string
Execute Method - returns a Matches collection containing a Match object(having properties firstindex and value) for each match found in string.

Replace Method - replaces the matched values in the given string by another value

Sample Example on Execute method.

```
'*******************************************
*************
Set regExpObject = New RegExp
search_string = "MS dhoni is very lucky cricketer"
regExpObject.Pattern = "lucky"

regExpObject.Ignorecase = true
regExpObject.Global = true

Set matches = regExpObject.execute(search_string)

For each match in matches
 print match.firstIndex & " - " & match.value
 Next
'*******************************************
*************
```

In above example we are trying to find the pattern "lucky" in the given string "MS dhoni is very lucky cricketer". We are also printing the position where the match is found.

6. **How to open any website(URL) in browser (IE,chrome, firefox) in QTP?**

You can use below code to open an url in QTP.

```
url = "www.google.co.in"
SystemUtil.Run "iexplore.exe" , url ,,,3
SystemUtil.Run "firefox.exe" , url ,,,3
SystemUtil.Run "chrome.exe" , url ,,,3
```

Above code will open url in all browsers.

In plain vbscript you can use below code to open a url.

```
Set o = createobject("wscript.shell")
o.Run "chrome.exe www.makaan.com"
o.Run "firefox.exe www.makaan.com"
Set o = nothing
```

www.ingramcontent.com/pod-product-compliance
Lightning Source LLC
Chambersburg PA
CBHW061029050326
40689CB00012B/2745